P9-ARV-382

Choosing What to Sell Online

A 4-Point Formula for Profitable Product Selection

Karen Brown

DEDICATION

To my newborn daughter:
Dharma Frances Brown

I can't imagine life without you now.

CONTENTS

ACKNOWLEDGEMENTS

I thank the Abraham-Hicks teachings for inspiring me.

Introduction

"What should I sell online?" That's one of the first questions one asks when first entering the world of e-retail. With that question comes an overwhelming number of choices. Literally millions of products are sold online every single day. The task of choosing just a few of those millions to sell can seem daunting.

This book will help you answer that question in a way that considers *your* personal goals and *your* situation. It will begin by reassuring you that there's plenty of money to be made in online selling. The seemingly overwhelming amount of information you're required to learn and process to become an e-retailer is merely the price of admission to earning a consistent and growing income in your spare time. This book will then introduce you to a formula that will help you wade through the millions of products you could possibly choose to sell online to find the one (or the several) that are perfect for *you* to sell right now. The value of this formula is that it was cultivated out of the lessons I learned over the past six years that I've spent buying and selling online. It steers you clear of many mistakes and focuses you on some of the considerations that will make your business soar. I feel confident that this book offers good guidance for new online sellers as well as for veteran sellers looking to change their business model and increase their sales.

Caution: This is <u>not</u> a book on product sourcing. There is one paragraph on product sourcing in this entire book and that's it. I intentionally wrote this book on the very narrow topic of choosing what to sell online so as to focus you on the importance of this choice to the success of your business. There are tons of books on product sourcing available on the Internet as well as hundreds of online articles.

So as not to disappoint those of you who are too Type-A to read the whole book and just want some quick ideas about what to sell online, I have included in Appendix A of this book a Hot Products List. This list includes the top 10 highest-demand products in 24 product categories on Amazon.com as of this writing.

You can use this information in several different ways. If you have these products at home, you now know you can sell them online for quick profits. Or, you could try to purchase these items from a vendor for re-sale. Still you could just peruse the categories to get a feel for what brands and products are popular and what you feel attracted to selling online

At the very end of this book in Appendix B you will find a fantastic offer for E-Retail Personal Sessions. Sometimes it just helps to talk to someone who's done what you're trying to do and have them give you one-on-one guidance specific to your personal situation. If after reading this book you feel you'd benefit from having this kind of guidance just know that affordable E-Retail Personal Sessions are available to you.

It is my wish that you find the content in this book realistic, useful, timely and written with care.

Enjoy.

Chapter One:

Hello

Who Am I?

My name is Karen Brown and I am a successful Amazon seller. I have operated a part-time business selling products occasionally on eBay and regularly on Amazon for about 6 years. I have a lifetime Amazon seller rating of 95% from 1,430 customer ratings as of this writing. In the past 3 years and while working a full-time job, I have grossed approximately $65,000 in sales on Amazon profiting approximately $48,000 after expenses. My main product line is new and used hardcover and paperback books. I also sell various health, beauty, household and home office products. I consider myself a seasoned Amazon seller whose made enough real money *(and enough costly mistakes!)* to be a useful guide to anyone wanting to learn to sell profitably online. It is my hope that you find the content of this book helpful, timely, well-written and easy to apply to your own situation.

Who Are You?

I know a little about who you are because all online sellers start at square one just like you are doing now. You are someone with a desire and a vision for a better life. You're tired of being broke or just getting by. Maybe you have a family to feed or you're barely making ends meet. Maybe you're just looking for an additional income stream should your full-time job disappear. Or, maybe you want to quit your job and do something more fulfilling and that makes you more money. You've heard that people can make a lot of money doing stuff online and maybe you've tried a few things. You've heard a little something about selling stuff online, too. You may even know some people who have sold stuff online and made money. Or, you may already be selling stuff online and just want to gather more information to improve your buying decisions. You came across this book and thought it might give you some good information. So you bought it. You made a good decision.

Once you begin seriously looking for products to sell online you go from "just thinking about it" to "just *doing* it." You become an entrepreneur specializing in the resale of new and/or used products to online consumers. You will have your own legitimate money-making business. You will be called a business-to-customer (B2C) seller since you will likely sell directly to the final consumer, at first, rather than to other businesses. You will popularly be known by the names "online seller," "e-retailer," "e-tailer," "retailer" or "dealer," to name a few. They all mean the same thing and are used interchangeably in this book. You will begin your business by buying new and/or used products to sell online from a manufacturer or another dealer like a distributor, liquidator, local retailer or other online seller. Or, you will spare yourself purchasing costs in the beginning and gather used products from your home and the homes of others you know to sell online. I like to call the latter scenario "repurposing product."

If you're like most new online sellers, you'll make some mistakes at first maybe even lose a little bit of money. But because you've purchased this book, you won't make as many mistakes or lose as much money as you could have! Soon the training wheels will come off and you'll see your profits go from a few dollars every couple weeks to a few hundred dollars every two or three weeks...then from a few hundred to a thousand each month. Before you know it, you're pulling in a thousand or more every two or three weeks and have nearly replaced your part-time job income...or maybe even your full-time job income. From there, the sky is the limit. Your life changes. With more money comes more freedom. You're home with the kids more. You're spending quality time with your mate. You're enjoying dinners out and mini-vacations. You're saving money. You're working your own hours from home and making good money doing something you enjoy. I think that no matter what images fill our dreams all of our dreams are essentially the same: to have more freedom and money to do what we want to do when we want to do it.

Online selling is a business that can give you just that kind of freedom and money.

Chapter Two:

Can I Really Make Money Selling Stuff Online?

The short answer to that question is a resounding "YES!" People all over the world make large amounts of money every day selling on sites like Amazon, eBay and Craig's List. According to the U. S. Census Bureau E-Stats E-commerce 2009 report (U. S. Census Bureau, 2011), "non-store retail e-sales" totaled approximately $117 billion in 2009. The U.S. Census Bureau's Quarterly Retail E-Commerce Sales Report for 1st Quarter 2011 (U. S. Census Bureau, 2011) indicates that e-commerce retail sales hit $46 billion in *just the first quarter* of 2011. These statistics imply that this year there could be approximately *$136 billion waiting to be earned by big and small businesses* through online retail sales! *$136 billion!* Sure, a large chunk of those consumer dollars will go to larger vendors like Wal-Mart, Zappos or Target, but at least a few billion of that amount will trickle down to reputable small business owners like you and me. A few thousand or a few hundred thousand of $136 billion to a small business owner is no small change!

What Does "Make Money" Mean to You?

You are wise to start your journey into the world of online selling with a clear understanding of what the phrase "make money" means to you. Everybody wants to "make money" online, but I haven't often heard people say *how much* money they actually want to make. It's important to know how much money you want to make because the amount you have in mind somewhat defines how you go about earning it. For example, if you want to make an extra $2k or $3k a month, you won't do it filling out surveys or through any other small-time hustle advertised on the Internet. To make several thousand dollars a month online *consistently*, you have to be moving some serious product and investing some serious time, energy and money in a legitimate business activity. The only limit to how much money you can make in e-retail is how much high-demand high-quality product you can buy to sell. So a great starting point would be to define in time and money what the phrase "make money" means to you. Note a specific dollar amount that you want to earn and a date by when you want to earn it consistently. In so doing, you can think about your date and income goal while reading this book and evaluate how realistic they are for you. So, take a few minutes and complete this sentence:

On or before [date], I will begin consistently making $_____ per _____ selling products online.

There - you've defined what "make money" means to you in writing. You have also defined what you're expecting your online retail business to do for you. Keep this statement in mind not only as you read this book, but during your entire time as an online seller. I recommend even posting it in a place where you can see it every day.

It Takes Time and Money to Make Money

You now know a lot of money can be made in selling products online and you have an income goal, so surely you're ready to get started! Not so fast. Before you go spending your potential earnings remember that it takes time and money to make money. Thankfully, online websites like Amazon and eBay make getting started in online retail sales relatively inexpensive and convenient. However, if you're starting on a shoestring budget of $100 or less or selling products around the house don't expect to make several thousand dollars in just a few weeks. I'm sure there are stories of just such a thing happening, but trust me when I say it's definitely not the norm.

At least on Amazon it takes time to make big money when you're starting off with small money. For example, if you want to net $2k per month after expenses selling on Amazon (and most other sites), then you're looking at an approximate initial investment of about $700 in used products or from $5k - $20k in new products depending on the products and assuming the products are in demand. Plus you're looking at about a week or more from listing the product for sale to getting paid from its sale. If you're starting off with $100 or less in new or used product then net earnings of $5 - $20 for new products and $50 - $150 for used products are reasonable expectations depending on the products and assuming you're selling products in demand.

Of course over time your initial investment will not be out-of-pocket. As you have more sales you will re-invest some or all of those sales proceeds to buy new product. But until you start having sufficient sales, your buying budget will come from your own cash. We'll talk more later about how I came up with those figures. Certainly these are just averages and exceptions exist for both scenarios. Yet, these averages are at least realistic. Having realistic expectations of not just the money you can earn, but the time and money it will take to earn the money you want to make is crucial to success in online retail sales.

Chapter Three:

Congratulations!
You're A Winner!

Plenty of people will say that you can't make money selling products online. But that is clearly not a true statement. It may be true that *they* can't make money selling products online, but that doesn't mean that *you* can't. So many new online sellers have rushed into online selling improperly prepared, shelling out big money on unprofitable or low-demand products only to see their investments go up in smoke. Or, they complain about the fees charged by Amazon or eBay and then quit. Or, they have been inattentive to customer service and so have allowed their seller ratings to drop and now no one will buy from them. Or, after making a few learning mistakes they just give up.

Any number of factors can be the reason why another person didn't succeed in online retail sales.

But their situation is not your situation. They are losers at the game of online retail. You, however, are already a winner! You've taken a wonderful first step by seeking guidance on choosing what products are right for you to sell online. Your choice to seek guidance shows some discernment, patience and careful treading, all of which are attributes that will make you a great and successful seller.

Listen to the Winners

My $48,000 in net sales over 3 years may seem a little impressive - especially considering I earned it selling low volume part-time. But there are hundreds if not thousands of Amazon and eBay power sellers making way more in one year or even *one month* than that $48,000 I made in 3 years. Seasoned successful sellers like me and these super-duper power sellers are the best resources for anyone serious about making big money in online retail sales. Seek out our guidance. Look into other books of how other successful sellers have made big money. Also look for books by successful online sellers that discuss the selling platform of your choice, i.e., eBay, Amazon, Craig's List, Buy.com, etc. Listen to and learn from the mistakes we have made. Be encouraged by our earnings and online reputations. Then set out on your own journey in e-retail keeping your own faith that you can and will succeed!

Chapter Four:

The Buy Right Formula

I have made a lot of mistakes (many of them expensive) over the years buying products to sell online. Lots of mistakes. But thankfully, I was failing forward because each new mistake I made taught me some important lesson about how to succeed in e-retail. I have affectionately come to call those lessons my "tuition" for learning to become a successful online seller. And I'm still learning - in fact, I don't think the learning ever stops. With each new product line or with each new vendor you work with or with each new deal or with each new and higher profit plateau you reach, there's some new lesson you have to learn to get to the next level. And the next level is always exciting because it usually means more money!

I have shortened all the lessons I've learned from all the mistakes I've made into a simple formula that I call, "The Buy Right Formula." I named this formula like so because if you think carefully about each point in this formula and apply it to your own selling situation, you will end up buying the right products, i.e., profitable products in good or better condition that sell fast. Choosing and then buying the right products practically guarantees a steady income and ever-increasing profit margins.

The Buy Right Formula is comprised of 4 points:

Compatibility + *Condition* + *Demand* + *Costs* = BUY!

Each of these 4 points is in some part personal to you. *Your* likes. *Your* opinions. *Your* money. *Your* selling preferences. *Your* style. *You.* No two people completing the Buy Right formula for their selling situation will get the exact same results. This formula is meant to be personalized. I often marvel at how some sellers believe, for example, that certain categories or types of products are such hot sellers that they should be purchased to the exclusion of all others. But I know for a fact that that's not true for everyone. Certainly some products, like iPads and WII consoles, sell like wildfire online. However, just because they sell like wildfire online doesn't mean they are the ideal product for *you* to sell *now*. The choice of what *you* should sell now is dependent on lots of things. And you will learn most if not all of these things through your use of the Buy Right formula in the pages that follow.

Keep in mind that learning the Buy Right formula and personalizing it to your situation is the first-step toward success in online selling. Your next step is to purchase the products you have chosen to sell. Product purchasing is covered under "Product Sourcing" – a topic not covered in this book. However, there are lots of great websites and reference materials that cover Product Sourcing extensively. Seek out these materials after you feel satisfied with your product selections.

So sit back. Get a pen for some notes. And get ready to learn a formula that will save you lots of time, protect you from lots of costly mistakes and make you lots of money!

Chapter Five:

Buy Right Formula Point #1: Compatibility

The first point in the Buy Right Formula is Compatibility. This point helps you to evaluate whether you and a particular product are a match. This may seem like an odd requirement for selecting products to sell online, but it's an important consideration that often goes overlooked. Compatibility considers the following four areas: interest, investment, manageability and permission. Let's look at each area closely.

Interest

You've probably read a million times that you should sell products you like. And I'm here to tell you that again for the millionth and one time. Sell things you like or use yourself!

One of the first mistakes new sellers make when choosing products to sell online is that they invest a lot of money on some product they don't really care about and haven't really researched with the expectation that they will make 300% profit or more on it. But sadly, they discover that the product won't sell and they end up stuck with a bunch of product for which they have no use and from which they can't get back their investment.

Buying products for resale that you already use or have some interest in saves you from this fate. When you already like or use a product, you have created a body of knowledge about the product that you can then use to assess condition, demand and costs - the remaining three points in the Buy Right Formula. In so doing, you protect your investment from uninformed buying decisions and yourself against unexpected profit losses.

Another reason to buy products for resale that interest you is because if you can't sell the products online, then you can absorb those products for personal use or sell them through other channels. Because of your interest level, you are in an ideal position to locate other vendors or buyers in your local area to whom you could possibly sell products that won't sell online. Or, you could sell them yourself at a local flea market or consignment shop.

Let's say you're still clueless about what kind of products you like that would also sell well online. Then choose products you would enjoy learning more about. For example, I am not a soap connoisseur, but I do love the Dr. Bronner's line of liquid soaps. I like the way they smell and the way they clean and nourish my skin. I use them regularly. For me, this is a great product to sell because I already like it and use it… and because I happen to know already that this brand of soap sells like wildfire online. My love for the Dr. Bronner's product line reveals that I favor natural and organic products - which is true. I enjoy organic fabrics and products made without synthetic ingredients. Organics and naturals are one focus area for my online selling. I enjoy researching and learning about new products in this area, so I am comfortable and successful buying and selling these kinds of products.

EXERCISE: Finding Products That Interest You Now

A great way to start choosing products that interest you is to peruse the Amazon product categories listing. Take a look at this Amazon screen-shot:

The drop-down box in the center lists all the categories of product Amazon sells on their website. To access the drop-down box, just go to the Amazon home page and look to the left of the empty search box at the top of the page where it says "All Departments." Next to that phrase is a grey and black arrow pointing down. Just click that arrow and the drop-down box appears listing all of the main categories of product Amazon has for sale. Then, just open each category and look through the sub-category headings. As you see headings that attract you, write them down. These will be the areas where you will focus your product selections.

Can I Make My Own Stuff And Sell It Online?

The short answer is "yes." Plenty of people are making and selling their own products online and doing very well. Just remember the Buy Right Formula's four points for choosing a product to sell online: compatibility, condition, demand and cost. Surely, you've got the first two knocked out - if you're making the products you must love them and, hopefully, you're making the products in good condition. That leaves demand and pricing. And since pricing is somewhat dependent on demand, we're really just left with demand.

That's where the long answer comes in. The choice whether to start out selling your own products depends on how fast you want to begin earning money. If you want to sell your own unknown products online you have to make people want them first. Drumming up demand in the beginning requires advertising and marketing costs that could be expensive and that could eat into your profit margin. When first starting out, consider choosing products to sell online that are already in demand. Then use the money you make from those sales to invest in advertising and marketing your own handmade creations.

Investment

The next area where you need to assess your own compatibility is with investment. Specifically, can you afford the initial investment required to buy the products you're interested in? Let's say you're looking to buy a few iPads to sell on eBay. As of this writing, a well-known liquidator website has one lot of four 64GB 1G iPads for sale at auction for $1,661.00. For some who just have their hearts set on selling electronics, that's more money than they have available for an initial investment. And don't think you'll buy just one iPad instead of four. Most distributors and liquidators sell their products in lots or require you to buy a minimum number of a product in order to buy at wholesale prices. And even if you do find a vendor willing to sell you just one iPad, you could pay close to retail for it and thereby eat up any profit margin you may have had.

A wise way to begin would be to first figure out how much you have to invest in product purchasing. If you're just selling stuff around your house then your initial investment for product will be zero. But don't think that lets you off the hook from reading this section! At some point you will exhaust your supply of free used stuff to sell online and will start seeking to buy used or new products for resale. At that point you will have to come back to this investment consideration. If you're buying new products to start, choose a product of which you can afford to buy at least 5-10 units. It's always better to buy in bulk because you get a lower price per unit which means a higher profit per unit. Later in this book, we'll talk a little more about knowing how much to pay for a product to be profitable. But for now, just make sure you have the money to comfortably invest in

5-10 units of a product at its <u>online selling price</u> plus the shipping amount showing on the selling platform of your choice. You won't buy the product for re-sale at this price – you're just making sure you have enough money to invest in more than 5-10 units once the math is all said and done.

Manageability

This consideration asks the question, "Can you move, lift, store and ship the products you've chosen to sell?" If you want to sell 42" flat screen TVs and have the money to buy 5-10 units of them, you will still run into trouble if you're living in a cramped studio apartment with no place to store them. Or if you're a lightweight selling those TVs by yourself, you may have some difficulty lifting or packaging the product for shipping. Here are other examples of things to think about when considering whether you can manage the product:

- How big is the packaged product?

- How much does it weigh?

- How much space will it take up in your home?

- Do you live in a place where boxes of product can be safely delivered and left if you're not home?

- Do you have room in your home to store the product for several weeks while you wait for it to sell?

- Do you have room in your car to pick up and drop off products from USPS, UPS, etc.?

- Do you have the equipment to test the products you want to sell, if necessary?

- Can you afford $200 - $300 to prepay postage, buy a postage scale, and stock shipping supplies?

- How much product can you handle at one time while managing other demands on your time?

Let this story be a lesson to you:

My first entry into the world of online selling was as an eBay seller back in 2006. The first product I chose to sell online was record albums. I can't remember now why I chose to sell albums back then. I knew they didn't have a lot of value, but I seem to remember liking the fact that I could buy so many of them for so cheap in the thrift stores in my area. So I bought several for resale. When I sat down to list them for sale online it occurred to me that I couldn't tell if they were any good because I didn't own a record player and I didn't know anyone who did. Also, I didn't really know or like any of the music I'd bought, so even if I did have a record player I wouldn't have wanted to listen to them. I ended up having to include in the description listing that I couldn't guarantee the quality of the albums - which had to have deterred at least a few sales. Still, however, I did manage to sell a few. When I went to ship the first one I learned that albums had to be shipped in a special kind of odd-sized corrugated packaging to ensure they didn't get damaged in transit. This packaging was expensive and somewhat hard to locate. Plus, the record covers were dusty which didn't fit in well with my neat and clean apartment. The records took a long time to sell and I didn't really have anywhere to put them. So they just sat in the way for months until I finally got tired of them and donated them back to the thrift store. The albums and I were tragically incompatible.

Permission

Great. You've chosen a product you like, you have the money to buy 5-10 units of the product upfront and you can manage the product in your living space. Sounds like you and this product are a match made in heaven, right? Not so fast. Before you take another step toward buying this product, you have to make sure you have permission to sell this product on the online selling platform of your choice.

Some selling platforms require you to receive special permission and adhere to certain guidelines before they will let you sell certain products on their website. For example, I was interested in reselling on Amazon several lots of software for sale by one of my favorite liquidators. Apparently the liquidator had just posted these lots for sale and the prices were amazing. I didn't even wonder whether I could sell software on Amazon because I'd seen software for sale on Amazon before. As I was doing my cost analysis (you will learn more about *Cost* later in this book) I went on the Amazon website to confirm the online selling price of the software. I was totally surprised to discover that I was required to ask Amazon for permission before I could sell the software online. At this point I'd been an Amazon seller for a few years so I thought I was green-lighted to sell just about anything. Turns out, however, that certain software products as well as several other categories of product require written permission or have strict guidelines governing their sale.

Take a look at Amazon's Content Guidelines at http://www.amazon.com/gp/help/customer/display.html?i e=UTF8&nodeId=15015801. These guidelines list different restrictions for different kinds of products. If you're selling on a different platform, such as eBay, be sure to seek out the content guidelines for that platform to ensure you are green-lighted to sell the products you want to sell.

Chapter Six:

Buy Right Formula Point #2:
Condition

The next point in the Buy Right formula is *Condition.*
Consumers don't spend $136 billion online each year to buy
junk…okay, maybe a few billion of that is allocated
specifically for junk! But even so consumers are still
expecting junk in good condition or at least the condition
described on the page where they purchased the junk.
Selling products online in poor condition can lead to
increased product returns, bad seller ratings, and huge profit
losses.

Product Condition v. Product Type

There is a difference between popular references to the
condition of the product and the product type. References

to the *condition* of the product are used most often by online sellers selling to the end consumer. Since your buyers may only see pictures of a product prior to purchasing, you will describe the condition of the product to them. Condition refers to a sensory assessment of any deterioration in look, sound, feeling, smell, taste or operation of a product from when it was brand new. Most selling platforms offer some variation of these four product conditions for you to classify the product generally: Collectible, New, Like New, Good and Acceptable. Then after you give the product a general product condition category, you will add an individual description of its current condition.

I will not give a description of each product condition here because these conditions are largely product-dependent. For example, the condition of a collectible antique tea set and a Like New Sony PlayStation 3 will differ immensely because the products differ immensely. Certain markings and indicators of value need to be included in the description for the collectible item that are not required for the Like New item. But to help you start learning the condition category standards for different products, check out the product Condition Guidelines on Amazon at http://www.amazon.com/gp/help/customer/display.html?nodeId=1161242. If you're not selling on Amazon, check your selling platform or other online resources to learn guidelines for each product condition.

References to product type are most used by dealers selling to other dealers in the product purchasing context. It refers to a classification given to a product by a vendor that includes not only condition but some idea of how and in what type of general situation it was last sold. As an online seller, you will give each individual product a condition prior to listing it for sale online. But as a dealer, a vendor selling to you will typically classify an entire lot of product as the same type - whether 2 units or a truckload. And then you will have to look at each individual product in the lot to determine its current individual condition.

These are not hard and fast rules, but rather a broad description of the differences between product condition and product type.

A Primer on Product Types

There are, in general, 4 product types you can buy or repurpose to sell online: Brand New, New-Surplus, Used and Salvage.

Brand New:
Products purchased directly from the manufacturer or a manufacturer's authorized distributor that have never been used and are still sealed in original packaging.

New-Surplus:
Excesses of unsold new product that have suffered a decrease in value. A large box store seller, like Best Buy or Macy's, would remove these products off the shelves and sell them to a liquidator who would then sell them in lots to smaller businesses like yours and mine. New-Surplus products are sometimes called overstock, closeouts, or shelf pulls. These three terms mean pretty much the same thing, except Shelf Pulls additionally describe product that has sat on brick-and-mortar store shelves unsold for a long time. So the manufacturer's packaging of these products may show some wear from handling or have discount stickers, etc.

Used:
Products that have been used by a consumer or vendor. Used products include returns, open-box specials, thrift store items and items from your own personal household. Used products also include refurbished products - products that have been repaired and are in good enough working condition to be re-sold.

Salvage:
Used products that are too damaged to be repaired or to serve their original purpose, but that can still be disassembled and sold for parts.

This is a broad overview of the different product types. To learn more about each type, a quick Internet search will give you tons of information. The vendor will also describe its product types on its website or in any additional selling information.

Product Condition Matters to Your Bottom Line

Product condition is included in the Buy Right Formula because condition directly impacts your earnings and your reputation as an online seller. Few consumers want products in bad condition - even products accurately described as being in bad condition. Two of few exceptions to that rule are buyers looking for certain salvage products and buyers looking for rare products. Salvage product buyers know already that the product is in bad condition, but they are hoping that some of the parts that form the product still have some value. Buyers of rare products will often buy products that aren't in the best condition just because they are so rare. Otherwise, the stark majority of online buyers want the best possible product in the best possible condition at the lowest possible price.

If you sell a product in bad condition you will likely lose money. When the buyer receives a product in bad condition (and especially if you didn't describe the product accurately as being in bad condition) the buyer will often return the product. If after you receive the product you discover it is in bad condition, you can't ethically re-sell the product. For example, maybe it was a malfunctioning electronics product that you didn't test before selling or a food product that turned out to be spoiled. Word of advice: if you buy a bunch of products at once, such as an auction lot, and you discover some of the products in the lot are in bad condition, just discard those particular products and cut your losses. Doing so may yield you fewer products to sell and increase your investment amount per product, but it will ultimately save you money you would have spent listing, storing and shipping a product that eventually would have been returned.

Another hazard of selling products in bad condition is that a buyer could express their dissatisfaction with your product by slamming your seller rating. For a new seller, this is not good. Seller ratings are like credit scores online. The better your score, the more people will buy from you. But the lower your score, the less sales you'll make because people won't trust you. And if your score is too low, the selling platform may even shut down your account.

Just remember: you are the best gauge of product condition. If you wouldn't buy a product in its current condition for your own use, then don't sell the product to someone else.

Sell New Products or Used Products in Great Condition

It's best to sell high-demand new products when at all possible. High-demand used products are also great to sell so long as they are in good or better condition. Collectibles are a highly specialized market. You will need to study them in order to know how to buy them. But if you're willing to put in the time and effort, selling collectibles online can also be quite lucrative.

This is Not a Book on Product Sourcing, But...

The actual process of buying the products you've decided to sell from reputable dealers at prices low enough for profitable resale is popularly called "Product Sourcing." As I mentioned earlier, this is not a book on product sourcing. However, here are a few key tips to whet your appetite:

Tip #1:
The best way to ensure a product is brand new is to buy directly from the manufacturer whenever possible. A quick Internet search on "the distribution chain" will give you the path a product travels to get to the final consumer. This path will give you some idea of the types of dealers you will call to inquire about buying product. But to start, simply call the manufacturer of a product you want to sell and ask them how you can buy their product at wholesale. Be sure to have your state reseller license available - most manufacturers and dealers will ask you for it before selling to you. If the manufacturer won't sell directly to you, often they will tell you who their distributors are and you can buy the product directly from them.

Tip #2:

Be leery of sites promising to give you "secret" or "members-only" lists of drop shippers and manufacturers. Some of these sites are scams. Some of these sites are legitimate, but may give you the names of dealers who are either selling low demand products or whose products are too expensive to buy to be at all profitable online.

Chapter Seven:

Buy Right Formula Point #3: Demand

The third point in the Buy Right Formula is *Demand*. Demand indicates what online consumers want to buy right now. You can then go buy those products for re-sale. Since buyers are already waiting to buy and assuming the other three points of the Buy Right Formula are satisfied you are <u>guaranteed</u> profitable sales.

I read once where an author compared sales strategy to fishing. The author explained that when fishing it's better to go to a full pond where the fish are already biting than to go to a quiet pond and try to create your own feeding frenzy. This instruction definitely applies to online selling. If you want to sell products online in order to create an immediate and growing income stream, it's better to sell online the products that consumers already want rather than try to entice consumers to want your unknown or low-demand products. The more consumers want a product, the faster it will sell and the higher the price it will command. Therefore, consumer demand for a product gives you insight into the current selling price of the product, the profit potential of the product and how fast the product is likely to sell. Demand also tells you what NOT to buy since low product demand directly correlates to low product sales. Demand is likely the most important point in the Buy Right Formula.

The Best Way to Discover the Hottest Selling Products Online

In the six years I've been selling online, I think the Amazon Bestsellers ranking system is by far the best gauge of demand for practically all new and most used products available for sale online. Even if you don't sell on Amazon, it still, arguably, gives the most accessible and useful information on consumer demand of any application. That's because it's free, timely, easy to read, and represents the online consumer spending choices of the leading e-retailer in the world: Amazon.com.

Internet Retailer, a leading business information provider for the e-commerce industry, in its <u>2011 Internet Retailer Top 500 Guide</u> (Internet Retailer, 2011) ranked Amazon as the #1 e-retailer in the U. S. and Canada. *Internet Retailer* uses the full-year online sales posted by e-retailers as the basis for its rankings. According to *Internet Retailer,* Amazon posted 2010 sales of $34.2 billion, far outpacing the $10.2 billion in online sales posted for #2 ranked Staples, Inc. This information suggests that the Amazon Bestsellers ranking system is a reliable indicator of general consumer demand for *most* products available for sale online today.

What the Amazon Bestsellers Ranking System is Not Good For

While Amazon is definitely the giant in e-retail it is not the favored selling platform for every single product in the universe. Collectibles, very unique items, and hard-to-find items in various categories are better sold on eBay, Craig's List or a website specializing in these kinds of products. Therefore, when trying to gauge demand for these kinds of products, eBay's market research programs may better suit your needs.

How to Use the Amazon Bestsellers Ranking System

Interpreting demand using the Amazon Bestsellers ranking system is fairly easy. Amazon gives every single product in every category on its website a numerical rank. The rank range begins with #1 as the highest rank and ends with the number of total listings in the category as the lowest rank. Many have wondered how Amazon calculates these rankings. But Amazon considers its calculations Super Duper Top Secret and refuses to reveal the underlying algorithms for its rankings to anyone. What Amazon does tell us in its help page is that the rank "is based on Amazon sales and is updated hourly to reflect recent and historical sales of every item sold on Amazon.com." (Amazon.com, 2011)

To illustrate the use of the Amazon Bestsellers ranking system, let's take a look at the Books category in this Amazon screen shot:

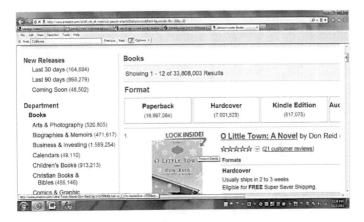

Draw your attention to the "Books" listing on the left side of the screen shot. There you will find a list of sub-categories of books available on Amazon by genre. If you look to the right of each sub-category in that list you will see a number in parentheses. That number indicates how many product listings Amazon has in its inventory for that particular sub-category. For example, let's look at the sub-category "Business & Investing." The number showing next to this sub-category is 1,589,254. This means Amazon has 1,589,254 book listings categorized as "Business & Investing", so the ranking of books in the "Business & Investing" category would range from #1 (highest demand) to #1,589,254 (lowest demand).

The Amazon Bestseller ranking for a particular product can be found in several places in the Amazon catalog, most notably in the Product Details section of the product's page. For example, one best-selling book in the "Business &

Investing" category is Daniel Kahneman's *Thinking, Fast and Slow*. Look at the product information listed for this book in the screen shot below:

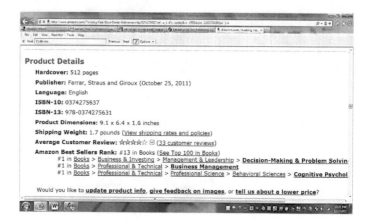

This book is ranked #13 in the "Books" category and #1 in several subcategories of the "Business & Investing" category. These high rankings tell us that this particular book is in high demand by online book consumers. Remember: <u>the lower the numerical ranking, the higher the demand for the product</u>. This book would be an excellent buy for re-sale assuming the three other points in the Buy Right formula are satisfied.

How High is Low?

Since low numerically-ranked products indicate high demand and fast sale, you may wonder how numerically high a ranking can be for it to still be considered low. In other words, at what point does a ranking become too numerically high to still indicate high demand? Amazon gives no guidance on how to find the tipping point in the Amazon Bestseller rankings where a product transitions from being in high demand to low demand. However, most seasoned Amazon sellers have some idea of how high low goes based on their selling experience in a product category.

I believe the majority of Amazon sellers will agree that a product ranked #100 in any main category, such as Books, is still a fast-selling, high-demand product. Many may also agree that a product ranked #1,000 in any category, though not as fast-selling as a #1 or a #100 product, will still sell at a fast enough pace to yield at least one or two daily sales. After a ranking of #1,000 however, the selling pace of a product starts to vary based on its product category and the number of products for sale in that category. For example, Amazon has approximately 31 million book listings total as of this writing. In contrast, it has approximately 2 million jewelry listings total. So a product ranked, say, #50,000, has a different demand in the Books category versus the Jewelry category because there are more books for sale in the Amazon catalog than there are jewelry products for sale. So to be the 50,000th ranked product on the Amazon Bestseller ranking system is still a high-demand ranking for the Books category, but not so much for the Jewelry category.

The 2% Buy Rule

As you develop selling experience with your products you will start to sense how fast a product sells at a particular ranking. But until then, I recommend you use the 2% Buy Rule to focus your buying on higher demand products. Here's how it works:

1. Find the total number of listings in your Amazon product category as described above.

2. Divide that number by 3.

3. Then multiply the new number by 2%.

This will give you a number that should somewhat reflect the top 2% range for that product category. I have you divide the total number by 3 because many of the products listed in the Amazon catalog are listed in duplicate. There are several reasons for this phenomenon that aren't really important to our discussion. But over the years while listing products I have found from 1 to sometimes 5 duplicate listings for the same product on Amazon. By dividing the total number of listings by 3, you receive a number that more accurately (but not perfectly) reflects how many actual products are in the category. So, using the Books category as an example:

1. There are 31 million listings in the Books category.

2. 31 million / 3 = 10,333,333

3. 10,333,333 * 2% = 206,000

Therefore, you should focus your buying for this category on products ranked #1 to #206,000. Based on my experience selling in the Books category, I can tell you that a book ranked #206,000 may take one to three weeks to sell versus the few minutes or so a book ranked #1 will take to sell. However, by focusing your buying in this range, you can be somewhat assured that your products ranked #1 to #206,000 will sell out, at most, within three to four weeks. Products closer to the #206,000 range that don't sell out within 3 weeks will likely drop in rank and fall out of the 2% range during that time.

Products Ranked Lower Than the Top 2% Are Still Profitable

The 2% Buy Rule does not prohibit you from buying products outside of the top 2% range. The benefit of the 2% Buy Rule is in focusing your product purchasing on products that are in highest demand and that are more likely to sell fast. You can buy products ranked lower than the top 2% and still be profitable. In fact, there are several good reasons to do so. For example, you may come across a product ranked #400,000 at a great purchase price that locks in an unbelievably high profit. In this instance, it makes sense to buy the lower ranked product because when it does sell you will get a very high profit.

Generally, slower selling products tie up your investment dollars longer thereby preventing you from using those dollars to invest in other products and make more money. So to make up for the time you are without the use of your investment dollars, it is wise to sell lower demand products only if they have a higher profit margin. For example, let's say you have a product ranked #1 and #100,000. The #1 ranked product will have multiple sales over the course of a few hours. This means that you will likely sell out of the product in a day or so and get your investment plus profit back almost immediately. You can then re-invest those earnings that same week into the same or another product and make more money.

Conversely, the #100,000 ranked product could take weeks or months to sell out depending on its category. This means that you will have to wait a month or more to get your investment plus profit back. Therefore to make up for lost time, it's wise to make sure that this product has a higher profit margin before you buy it. The higher profit margin should approximate or even exceed the dollars you would have made had you been able to get to your earnings from this product sooner and re-invest them.

Cut Your Losses at Six Months

Different sellers have different business models. Some buy low-demand products and let them sit until they sell. They live by the adage, "It's gotta sell at some point!" Others, like me, would rather keep products in inventory only for a few months, at most. In my first few years of online selling I used to buy low-demand products and let them sit forever. I no longer do that because even though a low-demand product has a high profit margin, if it sits online for more than three or four months, the profit margin starts to erode. Demand for the product drops and the product becomes very hard to sell. A good monthly practice is to clean out your aged product inventory. By "aged" I mean product you have had for sale online for longer than six months. If nothing else, you'll free up space, save on monthly listing costs or other fees and de-clutter your inventory.

No Need to Sell on Amazon to Use Its Rankings

You don't have to be an Amazon seller in order to use the Amazon Bestsellers ranking system. That's one reason this system is so great - it's free and accessible to anyone. Just run a search on Amazon for any product and the ranking for that product will appear in the product search results list. The ranking also appears in the Product Information section of the product page. In fact, Amazon posts its rankings for its products throughout its website. All you need to do is look up a product and you instantly have free access to some of the most valuable market research available online today.

Chapter Eight:

Buy Right Formula Point #4: Cost

The final point in the Buy Right Formula is *Cost*. It's exciting, for example, to find a compatible product in the best condition and that's ranked #1 on the Amazon Bestsellers list. However, if you can't buy that product at a price that allows you to be profitably competitive online then the product is still not a match for you. Therefore, cost is a deal-breaker that you absolutely must consider when choosing a product to sell online.

Cost - Defined

Cost refers to the <u>total amount</u> you will invest to buy a product and re-sell it profitably at its current online selling price. A product's current online selling price is created by its current demand – so to be competitive (i.e., get sales) you need to sell into the demand, which means you must be able to sell your product at or below its current online selling price. The only way you will know if you can do this profitably is by completing a simple cost analysis that takes into account the current online selling price, selling expenses, and profit. If the cost to sell this product is too high to make a profit, then you should <u>not</u> buy this product to sell online. If the profit potential of this product is too low to justify the time you will invest buying, listing, storing and shipping your product then you should <u>not</u> buy this product to sell online.

What Exactly is a Cost Analysis?

A *cost analysis* is a basic calculation you will use to *estimate* the total amount you must invest and the total profit you can expect to make from selling a particular product online. You can also adjust this basic calculation to predict the time it will take you to get back your investment and profit. This tool empowers you to make informed buying decisions and to reasonably predict how much you will make in product sales. The cost analysis along with the Amazon Bestsellers list are two tools that make choosing profitable products to sell online a whole lot easier.

How is a Cost Analysis Created?

There are as many different ways to create a cost analysis as there are online sellers who use them. That's because cost analyses are meant to be somewhat tailored to the user's selling preferences and product line experience. Some online sellers have a general cost analysis as simple as just dividing the online selling price by 3 and ensuring that their product costs and selling expenses don't equal more than 2/3rd of the selling price. Depending on the products they're selling, that could work effectively. Others, like me, prefer more accurate estimates and so use some kind of an equation to input specific information.

Here is a basic cost analysis for your use. This is an equation I have developed over time based on my experience selling various product lines on Amazon. This equation is meant as a conservative starting point for you. Over time as you learn more about how your product lines sell, you will adjust the equation to fit your needs and selling experience.

The basic cost analysis includes 4 variables: (1) the current online selling price, (2) product purchase costs, (3) selling and shipping expenses, and (4) a realistic profit margin. Each factor in the equation is represented by percentages so that you can apply the percentages to any dollar amount you want to use:

100%	=	50%	+	35%	+	15%
Selling Price		Product Purchase Price		Selling & Shipping Expenses		Profit

Selling Price:

The current online selling price. Consumer demand for the product created this price, so you will need to sell at or below this price in order to make sales. The percentage for this variable is 100% because the online selling price is always a composite of the other 3 variables. Even when you are purchasing products for your own use online or from box stores like Target or Wal-Mart, the price you pay at the register always includes at least these three variables.

Product Purchase Price:

The total amount you will give the vendor in order to purchase the products you want to sell online. This amount includes the total cost for all of the units, the cost to ship the products to you and any other buying fees charged by your vendor. This amount is set at 50%.

Selling & Shipping Expenses:

This is the total cost to sell your product on the selling platform of your choice (eBay, Amazon, Buy.com, etc.). This cost includes monthly fees, commissions, listing fees, etc. If you are using a storage facility or a fulfillment center (a place that stores and ships your products for you) then you would include costs for those services here. Remember to also include prepaid shipping costs, labels, envelopes and tape here, too. Once you've had a month or two of selling online, you will have a better idea of what percentage of your gross sales comprise your total overhead costs. You can then put that percentage here, too. For now the percentage for this variable is set at 35%.

Profit:

This is the amount you <u>realistically</u> expect to make from the sale of your products. For new products, a profit of 5% to 15% is the norm. But, you could get lucky and find a great deal that yields 20% profit or more. For used products the profit could be over 50%. When I sold books regularly, I consistently made profits of 200% or more, so high profits on used products are attainable. It's wise, however, to estimate conservatively on this number and then adjust it over time as you get a more realistic picture of what profits to expect. The percentage for this variable is set at 15%.

Again, the percentages appearing in this equation are variables based on my own selling experiences. You can and will change the percentage of any variable in this equation now or as your selling experience with your product increases. Just make sure to keep the estimates realistic and make sure the estimates for product purchase costs, selling and shipping expenses, and profit margin always equal 100% of the selling price.

How to Use a Cost Analysis to Estimate Expenses and Profit

A basic cost analysis is really easy to use. You simply fill in all the known factors of the equation and then let the equation calculate the unknowns for you. For example, let's say you have $100 to use as an initial investment. You *know* that your $100 is going to go toward purchasing product and paying for selling expenses. The total percentage for the Product Purchase and Selling & Shipping Costs variables total 85% (50%+35%).

100%	=	50%	+	35%	+	15%
Selling Price		Product Purchase Price		Selling & Shipping Expenses		Profit

Therefore, you ask the question, "$100 is 85% of what selling price?"

And you thought you'd never use your high school math again…

The equation looks like this:

1. Selling Price = Percent * What Number

2. Selling Price / Percent = What Number

And so...

1. $100 = .85x

2. $100 / .85 = $117.64

So $100 is 85% of what selling price? $117.64. And that was the hard part. The rest is easy. Just plug in the $117.64 into the Selling Price position and calculate the remaining variables by multiplying the percent times the selling price.

		(50% x 117.64)		(35% x 117.64)		(15% x 117.64)
$117.64	=	$58.82	+	$41.17	+	$17.65
Selling Price		Product Purchase Price		Selling & Shipping Expenses		Profit

With these dollar amounts what does this equation tell us? It tells us that we cannot sell our product for any less than $117.64 before expenses in order to get at least 15% profit margin. It tells us to budget $58.82 for product purchasing. It tells us to invest no more than $41.17 on selling and shipping expenses. And it tells us to expect $17.65 in profit. Not bad. If you plan to buy 10 units of product, we would divide all of these numbers by 10 to get the estimated per unit costs:

$5.88 per unit estimated for product purchasing

$4.11 per unit estimated for selling and shipping expenses

$1.77 per unit estimated for profit

= $11.76 per unit minimum selling price.

Do you see the benefit of the cost analysis? It estimates for you how much you will pay and how much you can profit from selling online at a competitive price. It also tells you when a product is not a good buy. For example, if you're interested in buying a product to re-sell on Amazon at its current selling price of $11.75 and it costs $9.00 to purchase one unit from the vendor then you know already that you cannot profit at least 15% off of this product on your existing investment without severely reducing your selling and shipping expenses. With this information, you can now decide whether to try to reduce those expenses and keep a 15% profit, leave those expenses intact and take a lesser profit, or decline to purchase this product at all.

If the math scares you, just go to the *Extras* tab on the *Choosing What to Sell Online* website (www.choosingwhattosellonline.com) to download this equation in an Excel spreadsheet. Then play around with the percentages to get a feel for how the cost analysis works.

What is a Sales Cycle?

The sales cycle is the period of time between when you first purchased or otherwise acquired the products you plan to sell online and when you actually received back in hand your total profit and initial product investment from the sale of all the product you purchased. Your sales cycle will vary depending on which selling platform you use, the current demand for your products, the time you spend processing your products, and the time it takes for your selling platform to pay you your earnings. The value of knowing the sales cycle is that it helps you predict how long and how fast it will take you to reach your income goals.

For example, I am an Amazon FBA (Fulfillment by Amazon) merchant. This means that after I buy my products for resale, I ship them to an Amazon warehouse where they are stored, picked, packed and shipped each time an order is placed. I do this because I hate fulfillment. I stored, packaged and shipped my own products for years and it just became too much of a hassle. So, I pay Amazon a small fee to do all of that for me and it is well worth the cost. With this information in mind, my sales cycle looks something like this:

1 day to place my order for products

1 day for the vendor to process and ship my order to me

3 days for my order to travel through the mail and arrive at my door

1 day for me to process and package my products for shipment to Amazon

3 days for my products to travel to Amazon through the mail

9 days for my products to sell out on Amazon

3 days for Amazon to direct deposit my earnings to my bank account

So based on this information, my sales cycle is approximately 21 days. Any number of things could happen to lengthen or shorten my cycle. My products may sell faster which may shorten the sales cycle. Or, my order could be delayed in shipping which may lengthen the sales cycle. But, in general, I can reasonably expect to get back my investment and profit in about 21 days from the date I first purchased the products to sell online.

Your sales cycle may likely be different. For example, if you're an eBay seller just selling products around your home, your sales cycle will shorten drastically because you need not make allowance for buying and receiving products from a vendor or waiting 3 days to receive payment. If you're an Amazon Marketplace merchant your sales cycle will also shorten because you don't have to ship your goods to Amazon. Your sales cycle will become more predictable as you gain more experience buying from different vendors and selling your products online.

The Value of Using a Sales Cycle

Knowing how long it will take to get paid from the sale of a product will help you figure out whether the product's profit potential is worth the time you will invest buying, storing, listing and shipping it. Using the profit amount from the cost analysis in the last section, there's a big difference between making $17.65 per hour and making $17.65 per month. Essentially, making $17.65 per hour is definitely worth your time and effort while making $17.65 per month doesn't even warrant getting out of bed. So it's important to estimate how much time it will take to get your investment and profit back so as to ensure you are receiving adequate value for your time.

Understanding the sales cycle is also critical to your setting realistic expectations about how fast you will make money from selling products online. Remember the time and money goal you set in Chapter 2? Adding the sales cycle to your cost analysis will tell you about how long it will take to start consistently earning whatever amount you identified in your personal goal. If you visit the *Extras* tab at the *Choosing What to Sell Online* website (www.choosingwhattosellonline.com), you will find an Excel spreadsheet that contains the basic cost analysis with a sales cycle equation included. Using this spreadsheet you can forecast out several cycles to see how long it will take you to reach a particular income goal.

Chapter Nine:

In Summary

You are now empowered by the guidance in this book to make informed and profitable choices about selecting products to sell online. Using the Buy Right Formula nearly *guarantees* that you will earn your fair share of the billions waiting to be spent in online products right now and thereby enjoy financial success as an online seller. The Buy Right Formula guides you to choose compatible products in good or better condition that are in high demand and that can be bought for resale at a price that gives you a good profit. In learning the Buy Right Formula you now have a valuable tool to help make your online retail business an outstanding success.

I invite you to peruse now the Hot Products List in Appendix A. This list gives the top 10 highest demand products in 24 product categories based on the Amazon Bestsellers rankings. This list is current as of this writing and changes hourly.

Also consider the E-Retail Personal Session offer in Appendix B. If after reading this book you desire one-on-one assistance, this offer may be just the ticket for you.

It was my goal and pleasure to try to make the content in this book realistic, useful, timely and written with care. If you feel this book was helpful to you, please visit the *Kudos* page at the *Choosing What to Sell Online* website (www.choosingwhattosellonline.com) and share your comments. You're also welcome to e-mail questions@choosingwhattosellonline.com should you have questions or comments.

I wish you all the best in your online selling career.

Welcome to the big leagues!

Appendix A:

The Hot Products List

Listed below are the (10) highest-demand products in 24 product categories on Amazon as of early Fall 2011. Products that appear in duplicate across different product categories were listed only once in the first category in which it appears.

The value of this list is to let you know what kind of products and product brands are in high-demand in each category so that you will have some sense of how and where to start focusing your buying activities. If you have any of these products in your home and you have no current use for them, these products should be the first products you sell online. Be sure to properly describe their condition. As I discussed in the *Demand* section of this book, products ranked #1 through #100 in any product category on the Amazon Bestsellers ranking are considered in highest-demand.

You can also use this list to get a feel for what product categories and brands to which you feel most attracted. Each category has sub-categories that can be viewed on the Amazon website as discussed in the *Interest* section of this book. Browsing those sub-categories will help you better narrow your focus to a particular product, product category or group of products you might like to sell online.

WARNING: This list changes frequently. If you want to know the highest-demand items in a given category right now, visit www.amazon.com and view the top-selling items in each category.

APPLIANCES

GE SmartWater MWF Refrigerator Water Filter, 1-Pack

Maytag UKF8001 Puriclean II Refrigerator Cyst Water Filter, 1-Pack

Cuisinart ICE-30BC Pure Indulgence 2-Quart Automatic Frozen Yogurt, Sorbet, and Ice Cream Maker

Eureka 71B Hand-Held Vacuum

Whirlpool 4396841P Side-by-Side Refrigerator, Push Button Fast Fill Water Filter, 2-Pack

Whirlpool 4396710P PUR Side-by-Side Refrigerator, Push Button Cyst Reducing Water Filter, 2-Pack

Cuisinart CSB-76BC SmartStick 200-Watt Immersion Hand Blender, Brushed Chrome

Hoover WindTunnel T-Series Rewind Upright Vacuum, Bagless, UH70120

Hoover SteamVac Carpet Cleaner with Clean Surge, F5914-900

Black & Decker TRO480BS Toast-R-Oven 4-Slice Toaster Oven

Arts, Crafts & Sewing

Brother CS6000i Sew Advance Sew Affordable 60-Stitch Computerized Free-Arm Sewing Machine

Scotch(TM) Thermal Laminating Pouches, 9 Inches x 11.4 Inches, 50 Pouches (TP3854-50)

50pc Lot Lampwork Murano Glass European Mix Beads - Compatible with Pandora, Chamilia, Troll, Biagi

Style SA156 Sewing Machine Bobbins for Brother - 10 Pack

Cricut 29-0002 Replacement Cutting Blades for Cricut Cutting Machines

3 Mil Clear Letter Size Thermal Laminating Pouches 9 X 11.5 (Qty 100) (03NPSM)

Brother XL2600I Sew Advance Sew Affordable 25-Stitch Free-Arm Sewing Machine

Cricut 29-0386 12-by-12-Inch Tacky Cutting Mats with Measurement Grids, Set of 2

knit, Swirl! Uniquely Flattering, One Piece, One Seam Swirl Jackets; Foreword by Cat Bordhi by Sandra McIver (Hardcover - May 15, 2011)

Melissa & Doug Friendship Stamp Set

Automotive

Garmin Portable Friction Mount

Garmin nüvi 1350LMT 4.3-Inch Portable GPS Navigator with Lifetime Map & Traffic Updates

Garmin nüvi 1450LMT 5-Inch Portable GPS Navigator with Lifetime Map & Traffic Updates

Garmin nüvi 255W 4.3-Inch Widescreen Portable GPS Navigator

4.3" EVA Case for Garmin Nuvi 265wt 1300 1350 1370t GPS

ChargerCity GPS Garmin Nuvi Windshield ball & socket suction cup mount & Bracket unit holster bundle for Garmin nuvi 200 200W 205 205W 250 250W 255 255W 260 260W 265T 265WT 270 275T 285 285w 285t 285wt (Direct Replacement Warranty)

TomTom XL 335SE 4.3-Inch Widescreen Portable GPS Navigator (Factory Refurbished)

TomTom GPS Dashboard Mount for TomTom GPS Navigators

Belkin BE112230-08 12-Outlet Home/Office Surge Protector with Telephone and Coaxial Protection

ContourHD Camera

BABY

Pampers Baby Dry Diapers Economy Pack Plus, Size 4, 192 Count

Pampers Sensitive Baby 3x Wipes Refills, 192 Count Packages (Pack of 4)

Playtex Diaper Genie II Refill (Pack of 3)

Huggies Snug & Dry Diapers, Size 4, 140 Count

Pampers Soft Care Scented 10x Wipes, 720 Count

Luvs Ultra Leakguards Diapers, Size 4, 204-Count

Pampers Cruisers Diapers Economy Plus Pack, Size 4, 160 Count

Huggies Natural Care Baby Wipes, Fragrance-Free, Refill, 216-Count Pack (Pack of 3)

Pampers Swaddlers Sensitive Diapers, Size 3, 156 Count

Vulli Sophie the Giraffe Teether

BEAUTY

Rogaine for Men Hair Regrowth Treatment, Easy-to-Use Foam, 2.11 Ounce, (3 month supply)

Loving Naturals SPF 30 Sunscreen Zinc Oxide 5 Oz. UVA/UVB Vegan

Farouk CHI 1 Inch Ceramic Flat Hairstyling Iron

Moroccanoil, 3.4-Ounce Bottle

Millenium Tanning New Paint It Black Auto-darkening Dark Tanning Lotion, 50X, 13.5-Ounce

Olay Professional Pro-X Advanced Cleansing System

Nioxin Intensive Therapy Recharging Complex, 90 Count

Revlon RV544 1875 Watt Tourmaline Ionic Lightweight Dryer, Silver/Black

Cellular Support 60 Softgels

Salicylic Acid 20% Gel Peel, 30ml (Professional)

BOOKS

Go the F**k to Sleep by Adam Mansbach and Ricardo Cortés

The Hunger Games by Suzanne Collins and Carolyn McCormick

A Little Death In Dixie by Lisa Turner

The Help (Movie Tie-In) by Kathryn Stockett

Water for Elephants: A Novel by Sara Gruen

Cotillion by Georgette Heyer

Maid for the Billionaire (Book 1) (Legacy Collection) by Ruth Cardello

Catching Fire: The Hunger Games #2 by Suzanne Collins

This Fine Life: A Novel by Eva Marie Everson

Surrender the Heart (Surrender to Destiny) by Marylu Tyndall

CELL PHONES & ACCESSORIES

Motorola Vehicle Power Adapter micro-USB Rapid Rate Charger

Three LCD Screen Guards / Protectors for Apple iPod Touch 4 / 4G / 4th Gen

5-Pack Premium Reusable LCD Screen Protector with Lint Cleaning Cloth for Apple iPhone 3G 8GB 16GB [Accessory Export Packaging]

Fosmon Transparent Clear Screen Protector for iPhone 4 4G HD with Lint Cleaning Cloth - 3 Pack

3-Pack HTC EVO 4G Sprint Combo Screen Protector for HTC EVO 4G Sprint

Motorola SPN5504/SKN5004A micro-USB Home and Travel Charger

Stereo Headset /w Microphone for Apple iPhone 3G (White)

Motorola SB6120 SURFboard DOCSIS 3.0 eXtreme Broadband Cable Modem

White Sync & Charge USB Cable for Apple iPhone 3G / Apple iPhone 3GS

Car Charger for Apple iPhone 4 (Black)

ELECTRONICS

Kindle, Wi-Fi, Graphite, 6" Display with New E Ink Pearl Technology

Kindle Lighted Leather Cover, Black (Fits 6" Display, Latest Generation Kindle)

HDMI Cable 2M (6 Feet)

Transcend 16 GB Class 10 SDHC Flash Memory Card TS16GSDHC10E

Apple iPod touch 8 GB (4th Generation) NEWEST MODEL

Apple iPod touch 32 GB (4th Generation) NEWEST MODEL

Motorola Vehicle Power Adapter micro-USB Rapid Rate Charger

Three LCD Screen Guards / Protectors for Apple iPod Touch 4 / 4G / 4th Gen

BlueRigger High Speed HDMI Cable with Ethernet 6.6 Feet (2m) - Supports 3D and Audio Return [Latest Version]

5-Pack Premium Reusable LCD Screen Protector with Lint Cleaning Cloth for Apple iPhone 3G 8GB 16GB [Accessory Export Packaging]

GROCERY & GOURMET FOOD

Coffee People, Donut Shop K-Cups for Keurig Brewers (Pack of 50)

eKobrew Cup, Refillable K-Cup For Keurig K-Cup Brewers

Playtex Diaper Genie II Refill (Pack of 3)

Seventh Generation Baby Wipes Refills, Chlorine Free and Unscented, 70-Count Packs (Pack of 12) (840 Wipes)

ZICO Pure Premium Coconut Water, Natural, 11.2-Ounce Tetra Paks (Pack of 12)

Seventh Generation Chlorine Free Baby Wipes, 350 Unscented Wipes

Nutiva Organic Extra Virgin Coconut Oil, 15-Ounce Tubs (Pack of 2)

Vita Coco 100% Pure Coconut Water, 11.1-Ounce Containers (Pack of 12)

Timothy's World Coffee, Colombian Decaffeinated Medium K-Cups for Keurig Brewers (Pack of 50)

Miracle Noodle Shirataki Angel Hair Pasta, 7-Ounce Packages (Pack of 6)

HEALTH & PERSONAL CARE

USP Labs Oxy Elite Pro, 90-capsule

Philips Norelco 7310XL Men's Shaving System

Braun Clean & Renew Refills (3 Pack)

Philips Sonicare ProResults HX6013 Brush Head Standard 3pk

Optimum Nutrition 100% Whey Gold Standard, Double Rich Chocolate, 5 Pound

Lansinoh 20435 Breastmilk Storage Bags, 25-Count Boxes (Pack of 3)

Philips Sonicare Hx7002/30 E-series Replacement Brush Head, White

Waterpik Ultra Water Flosser

EatSmart Precision Digital Bathroom Scale w/ Extra Large Backlit 3.5" Display and "Step-On" Technology

Omron HJ-112 Digital Pocket Pedometer

HOME, GARDEN & PETS

Black & Decker HPB18-OPE 18-Volt Slide Pack Battery For 18-Volt Outdoor Cordless Power Tools

Vinturi Essential Wine Aerator

Weber 7553 Premium Cover for Weber Genesis Gas Grills

Weber 7416 Rapidfire Chimney Starter

Weber Style 6445 Professional-Grade Stainless-Steel 3-Piece Barbeque Tool Set

Emergency Fire Starter

Krups 203-42 Fast Touch Coffee Grinder, Black

Grill Daddy GD12952c Grill Daddy Pro Grill Brush

GE 13-Watt Energy SmartTM - 8 Pack - 60 watt replacement

Black & Decker AF-100-3ZP 30-Feet 0.065-Inch Line String Trimmer Replacement Spool, 3-Pack

INDUSTRIAL & SCIENTIFIC

AmazonBasics Toslink Digital Audio Optical Cable (6 Feet/1.8 Meters)

DEWALT DC725KA 18-Volt Cordless Compact Hammer Drill/Driver

Smith's PP1 Pocket Pal Multifunction Sharpener

Bosch PS20-2A 12-Volt Max Lithium-Ion Pocket Driver with 2 Batteries

Gerber 31-000751 Bear Grylls Survival Series Ultimate Knife, Serrated Edge

AO Safety 90541 WorkTunes AM/FM Hearing Protector with Digital Tuning and MP3 Input

Dewalt DPG82-11C Concealer Clear Anti-Fog Dual Mold Safety Goggle

DEWALT DCD760KL 18-Volt 1/2-Inch Cordless Compact Lithium-Ion Drill/Driver Kit

Above All Forearm Forklift Lifting and Moving Straps, Orange

Mtech Extreme Tactical Folding Pocket Knife,With Aluminum Handle Knives Black

JEWELRY

14k 8.75mm Flat Figaro Chain Length 22"

Trion:Z Wrist Bracelet

11.75mm, 14 Karat Yellow Gold, Beveled Curb Chain - 22 inch

New Trent CD-3800 Digital Ultrasonic for Jewelry, Eyeglass, and Dentures Cleaner

Certified 18k White Gold, Princess-Cut, Diamond 4-Prong Stud Earrings (2 cttw, H-I Color, SI1-SI2 Clarity)

1/2 ct. Blue - I1 Round Brilliant Cut Diamond Earring Studs in 14K White Gold

Phiten Tornado Titanium Necklace

Phiten Star Necklace

Men's 14k White Gold 6mm Comfort Fit Wedding Band Ring, Size 11.5

14k Yellow Gold 8.5-9mm White Freshwater Cultured AA Quality Pearl Necklace, 60"

MOVIES & TV

True Grit (Blu-ray/DVD Combo + Digital Copy) Starring Matt Damon and Jeff Bridges (2011)

Back to the Future: 25th Anniversary Trilogy (+ Digital Copy) [Blu-ray] Starring Michael J. Fox, Christopher Lloyd, Lea Thompson, et al. (2010)True Grit Starring Matt Damon and Jeff Bridges (2011)

True Blood: The Complete Third Season Starring Anna Paquin, Stephen Moyer, Sam Trammell and Ryan Kwanten (2011)

ESPN Films: 30 for 30 Limited Edition Collector Set Starring Allen Iverson, Muhammad Ali, Jimmy The Greek, et al. (2011)

Pirates of the Caribbean: On Stranger Tides (Five-Disc Combo: Blu-ray 3D / Blu-ray / DVD / Digital Copy) Starring Johnny Depp, Penélope Cruz, Ian McShane and Geoffrey Rush

Harry Potter and the Deathly Hallows, Part 1 Starring Daniel Radcliffe, Rupert Grint and Emma Watson (2011)

Star Trek: Original Motion Picture Collection (The Motion Picture / The Wrath of Khan / The Search for Spock / The Voyage Home / The Final Frontier / The ... Captains Summit Bonus Disc) [Blu-ray] Starring William Shatner, Leonard Nimoy, DeForest Kelley, et al. (2009)

The King's Speech Starring Colin Firth, Helena Bonham Carter, Geoffrey Rush, et al. (2011)

Zumba Fitness Total Body Transformation System DVD Set

P90X: Tony Horton's 90-Day Extreme Home Fitness Workout DVD Program

MUSIC

Dream With Me by Jackie Evancho (Audio CD - 2011)

21 by Adele (Audio CD - 2011)

Il Volo by Il Volo (Audio CD - 2011)

Born This Way (Special Edition) by Lady Gaga (Audio CD - 2011) - Special Edition

Revelator by Tedeschi Trucks Band (Audio CD - 2011)

The Book of Mormon by Trey Parker, Robert Lopez, Matt Stone, Stephen Oremus and Josh Gad (Audio CD - 2011) - Cast Recording

Ukulele Songs by Eddie Vedder (Audio CD - 2011)

19 by Adele (Audio CD - 2008)

Sigh No More by Mumford & Sons (Audio CD - 2010)

A Treasure (CD) by Neil Young (Audio CD - 2011)

MUSICAL INSTRUMENTS

Professional Cable ST35MM-06 Stereo 3.5mm 6-ft M/M Cable - Black

Snark SN-2 All Instrument Clip-On Chromatic Tuner

Snark SN-1 Tuner

Musician's Gear Tubular Guitar Stand Black

RCA AH16100SN 16-Gauge Speaker Wire (100 Feet)

Cables Unlimited AUD-1100-06 6-Feet 3.5MM Male to Male Stereo Cable

Nady MPF-6 6-Inch Clamp On Microphone Pop Filter

Planet Waves Assorted Pearl Celluloid Guitar Picks, 10 pack, Medium

M-Audio SP-2 US65010 Sustain Pedal Piano Style Sustain Pedal for Keyboards

3 RCA to USB Cable

OFFICE PRODUCTS

Canon CLI-221 4-Color Value Pack
(Black/Cyan/Magenta/... (2946B004) in Retail Packaging

CaseCrown Apple iPad 2 Bold Standby case (Black) for the
Apple iPad 2 Wifi / 3G Model 16GB, 32GB, 64GB

Canon PIXMA MG5220 Wireless Inkjet Photo All-In-One
(4502B017)

Snugg iPad 2 Leather Case Cover and Flip Stand for the
Apple iPad 2 (Black)

Canon PG-210XL Cartridge (Black) in Retail Packaging

Canon PGI-220 Cartridge Combo Pack - Triple Pack (Black)

Canon PGI-225 BK/ CLI-226 C,M,Y Cartridge 4 Pack
Value Pack (4530B008) in Retail Packaging

HP 60 Ink Cartridge in Retail Packaging, Combo Pack
(CD947FN#140)

Case Logic EHDC-101 Hard Shell 2.5-Inch Portable Hard
Drive Case (EHDC-101Blue)

Case Logic QHDC-101 Portable EVA Hard Drive Case
(Black)

SOFTWARE

Microsoft Office 2010 Home & Student (Disc Version) -
Windows 2003 Server / 7 / Vista / XP

QuickBooks Pro 2011 - Windows 7 / Vista / XP

Portal 2 - Mac OS X, Windows Vista / XP

Adobe Photoshop Elements 9 (Win/Mac) - Mac OS X, Windows 7 / Vista / XP

McAfee Total Protection 2011 3-User - Windows 7 / Vista / XP

Adobe Photoshop Lightroom 3 - Mac OS X, Windows 7 / Vista / XP

The Sims 3: Generations - Mac OS X 10.5 Leopard / Intel, Windows Vista / XP

Duke Nukem Forever - Windows 7 / XP

Norton 360 5.0 1-User/3PCs - Windows 7 / Vista / XP

Kaspersky Internet Security 2011 3-User - Windows 7 / Vista / XP

SPORTS & OUTDOORS

Garmin Forerunner 305 GPS Receiver With Heart Rate Monitor

Rothco 550lb. Type III Paracord

CamelBak BPA-Free Better Bottle with Bite Valve

Omron HJ-112 Digital Pocket Pedometer

INSANITY: 60-Day Total Body Conditioning Workout DVD Program

Stearns Kids Puddle Jumper Deluxe Life Jacket

Zumba Fitness Exhilarate: The Ultimate Experience DVD Set

Polar Insulated Water Bottle

Klean Kanteen Stainless Steel Water Bottle

Weber 7553 Premium Cover for Weber Genesis Gas Grills

TOOLS & HOME IMPROVEMENT

Black & Decker HPB18-OPE 18-Volt Slide Pack Battery For 18-Volt Outdoor Cordless Power Tools

Belkin Mini Surge Protector Dual USB Charger

Smith's PP1 Pocket Pal Multifunction Sharpener

RCA ANT1650 Flat Digital Amplified Indoor TV Antenna

GE 13-Watt Energy SmartTM - 8 Pack - 60 watt replacement

PUR CRF-950Z 2-Stage Water Pitcher Replacement Filter, 3-Pack

Contech Electronics CRO101 Scarecrow Motion-Activated Sprinkler

Whirlpool 4396841P Side-by-Side Refrigerator, Push Button Fast Fill Water Filter, 2-Pack

Brita 24-Ounce Bottle with Filter, Twin Pack

Belkin BE112230-08 12-Outlet Home/Office Surge Protector with Telephone and Coaxial Protection

TOYS & GAMES

Syma S107/S107G R/C Helicopter (Various Colors)

25 Ultra Pro 9 Pocket Page Protectors Fits 3-Ring Binder for Baseball and Other Sports Cards!

Insect Lore Live Butterfly Garden

Baby Einstein Take Along Tunes

Rory's Story Cubes

Stomp Rocket Jr. Glow Kit

Step2 WaterWheel Activity Play Table

Perplexus Maze Game by PlaSmart, Inc.

Baby Einstein Bendy Ball

Cloud b Twilight Constellation Night Light, Turtle

VHS

The Lion King (A Walt Disney Masterpiece) [VHS] Starring Matthew Broderick, Jeremy Irons, James Earl Jones, et al. (1995)

The Little Mermaid (Fully Restored Special Edition) (Disney's Masterpiece) [VHS] Starring Jodi Benson, Samuel E. Wright, Rene Auberjonois, et al. (1998)

Cinderella (Walt Disney's Masterpiece) [VHS] Starring Ilene Woods, James MacDonald, Eleanor Audley, et al. (1995)

Peter Pan (Fully Restored 45th Anniversary Limited Edition) (Walt Disney Masterpiece Collection) [VHS] Starring Bobby Driscoll, Kathryn Beaumont, Hans Conried, et al. (1998)

101 Dalmatians (Walt Disney's Classic) [VHS] Starring Rod Taylor, Betty Lou Gerson, J. Pat O'Malley, et al. (1992)

The Jungle Book (Fully Restored 30th Anniversary Limited Edition) [VHS] Starring Phil Harris, Sebastian Cabot, Louis Prima, et al. (1997)

Tae-Bo Workout: Instructional and Basic (Tae-Bo: The Ultimate Total Body Workout for Men & Women) [VHS] Starring Billy Blanks (1998)

The Little Mermaid II - Return to the Sea (Walt Disney Pictures Presents) [VHS] Starring Tara Strong, Pat Carroll, Jodi Benson and Samuel E. Wright (2000)

Lady and the Tramp [VHS] Starring Barbara Luddy, Larry Roberts, Peggy Lee and Bill Thompson (1998)

The Lion King II: Simba's Pride [VHS] Starring Matthew Broderick, Neve Campbell, Andy Dick, et al. (1998)

VIDEO GAMES

L.A. Noire by Rockstar Games - PlayStation 3 & Xbox 360

AmazonBasics High Speed HDMI Cable (6.5 Feet / 2.0 Meters) - Supports Ethernet, 3D, and Audio Return

PlayStation 3 160 GB by Sony - PlayStation 3

LEGO Pirates of The Caribbean mini-figurine by Amazon

inFAMOUS 2 by Sony Computer Entertainment - PlayStation 3

PlayStation 3 Dualshock 3 Wireless Controller (Black) by Sony Computer Entertainment - PlayStation 3

The Legend of Zelda: Ocarina of Time 3D by Nintendo - Nintendo 3DS

Zumba Fitness by Majesco Sales Inc. - Nintendo Wii

Halo Reach by Microsoft - Xbox 360

Just Dance 2 by UBI Soft - Nintendo Wii

WATCHES

Suunto Core Wrist-Top Computer Watch

Cartier Ballon Bleu Medium 18k White Gold Watch WE9006Z3

TAG Heuer Men's WAF1110.BA0800 2000 Aquaracer Quartz Watch

Invicta Men's 0764 II Collection Black Dial Black Leather Watch

Michael Kors Women's Watch MK5039

Baume & Mercier Men's 8749 Hampton Square Titanium Watch

Citizen Men's BL5250-02L Eco-Drive Perpetual Calendar Chronograph Watch

Invicta Men's 8928OB Pro Diver Two-Tone Automatic Watch

Casio Men's PAW2000-1CR Pathfinder Digital Multi-Function Resin Band Watch

Ironman Global Trainer GPS Watch with Digital 2.4 Heart Rate Monitor

Appendix B:

The E-Retail Personal Session

Sometimes just talking to someone who is already in the business you want to be in helps a lot. In this day and age of impersonal electronic communication, hearing guidance in the human voice of another can be comforting an extremely helpful in understanding your next steps.

E-Retail Personal Sessions give you one-on-one, voice-to-voice help in choosing what to sell for your online retail business. If you have other questions not covered in this book or would like clarification on portions of this book as they relate to your personal situation, this is a great opportunity to talk to me in person and get your questions answered.

If you would like more information on the E-Retail Personal Sessions, just visit the *E-Retail Personal Session* tab at the *Choosing What to Sell Online* website (www.choosingwhattosellonline.com).

BIBLIOGRAPHY

Amazon.com. (2011). Amazon.com Help: What Amazon Bestsellers Rank Means. Retrieved June 18, 2011, from Amazon.com:
http://www.amazon.com/gp/help/customer/display.html?nodeId=525376

Internet Retailer. (n.d.). The Top 500 List - Internet Retailer. Retrieved June 19, 2011, from Internet Retailer: http://www.internetretailer.com/top500/list/

U. S. Census Bureau. (2011, May 12). Monthly & Annual Retail Trade. Retrieved June 19, 2011, from U. S. Census Bureau: http://www.census.gov/retail/

U. S. Census Bureau. (2011, June 2). U. S. Census Bureau E-Stats Main Page. Retrieved June 19, 2011, from U. S. Census Bureau:
http://www.census.gov/econ/estats/2009/table6.pdf

###

I hope you found this book useful, timely and well-written.

ABOUT THE AUTHOR

Mother. Writer. Internet Entrepreneur. Native Virginian. Bibliophile. Optimist. Runner. Libra. Professional Speaker. Health Nut. Free Spirit. Traveler. Adventurer. Washington Redskins Fan. Deep Thinker. Social Butterfly.

Connect With Me Online:

Website: www.choosingwhattosellonline.com
E-Mail: questions@choosingwhattosellonline.com
Twitter: http://twitter.com/ShaktiWrites

11813454R00046

Made in the USA
Charleston, SC
22 March 2012